The Seafarer

Matthew Hollis & Norman McBeath

HAZEL PRESS

First published in 2024
by Hazel Press
22 Coneygar Close, Bridport, Dorset DT6 3AR
www.hazelpress.co.uk

A CIP record for this title is available from the British Library

Design / Typography: Dale Tomlinson
Typeface: Arno Pro
Cover Photograph: *Seafarer I*, Norman McBeath

ISBN 978-1-7394218-5-4

First Edition

Printed in England by Anglian Print Ltd, Beccles, Suffolk, on 100% recycled paper, using vegetable-based inks. Anglia Print has gained the following certifications:

Foreword

WE DO NOT KNOW who the seafarer was. We do not know when his tale was told, nor from which coastline it came. But come it did, in lines inscribed across four pages of the *Exeter Book* (81^{v}–83^{r}) by clerics in the tenth century. The origins of the poem are certainly older, but it retains such immediate force and presence that more than a millennia after its composition it is possible to be transported by it still.

Mæg ic be me sylfum soðgied wrecan, the poem opens, which in Ezra Pound's famed, first translation of the modern era reads, 'May I for my own self song's truth reckon': the singer's hush of an expectant crowd, the poet's call for attention, the wondrous sounding *siþas secgan,* 'experience to relate'. And for a moment, silence falls. Then the storm pours in.

Wild words sweep in off salt waters, a blunt wind bullies and booms. Winter presses quickly and deep, *forste gebunden* (frost-bound) and *caldum clommum* (cold-gripped), roaring across half-frozen seas. Wave-surge and chilled chains, hardened hawser and sleepless watch, blizzards barrelling in from the north.

But conditions are even more severe within. No sooner do we learn of these elemental dangers then we come to understand an inner human drama. We are told of *earfoðhwile* (literally 'trouble-while', a time of hardship) and *breostceare* ('breast-care', heartache), and are left in no doubt that outer maelstrom is a mirror to turmoil within. The seafarer is alone on an empty and threatening ocean, his scant company the birds that the winter weather is soon to cast up. And not just *alone*, but something far more punishing still: he is *cast out*. And it's this sole – and surely *soul* – existence that drives *The Seafarer* through the powerful Old English word, *wraecca*: *n.* 'one driven from his own country, a wanderer in foreign lands, an exile, a stranger, pilgrim' (Bosworth Toller); 'fugitive, outcast' (Clark Hall); 'wretch' (Sweet).

'Exile' is a deep and self-examining word at any moment in history, but in Anglo-Saxon times it was especially weighted. Society ran in small units in which survival depended upon fidelity to a *cyning* or king or lord, who in return provided protection from a threatening world beyond, as well as granting social standing to members within. To live outside the *cynn* is to live in peril: to exist on your wits, with no one but yourself to save you. So it is with poignancy that the seafarer scans the waves toward the shore where *þe him on foldan fægrost limpeð* – those 'whose lot is cast most happily on land' (Ida Gordon) – are observed in a state of untroubled contentment. The poem wants to say something about the unexamined life: about those who have never risked the community of the soil for the isolation of the sea; those who know only the bounty of spring but not the relentless winter of the ocean; those who accept the limits granted them, and those who pursue a transgressive pilgrimage.

To be the *winter wunade* – to be the seafarer – is to pose ourselves a series of troubling questions.

In what way should we live our life: from the security of the known, or on the risky path of revelation?

What should our obligations be: to depend upon others, or survive in our way alone?

Is suffering inevitable in order to arrive at enlightenment?

And what of our greater purpose: is it to live, or merely to exist?

Ancient as these questions are, such examinations matter no less to us today than ever they did to the seafarer. Now, in the times we face. Now, when our planetary weather grows dangerously wild. Now, as our kinship to society comes under strain. Now, as we desire to find a life that we can call sustainable: one in tune with natural elements, one that commands itself ever more urgently to hear again, as the Anglo-Saxons did, the spirit-music of land and wind and sea.

The Seafarer is a perilous work to translate, so varied in tone that it's thought to have been composed in different instalments by different writers at different times. The opening half is the earliest, while the conclusion is considered the extension of a later scribe, leading to disagreements about how long the poem should actually *be*: most translators give it at 124 lines but others have ended it twenty lines sooner. It contains attitudes toward the sea that appear so contradictory that it's been suggested that the poem is not the monologue we generally take it for, but a dialogue between *two* sailors, older and younger. Other readings believe the variety in voice stems from the confusion of two discrete texts by wayward clerics, with the claim that somewhere along the line the wrong tail may have been stuck on the wrong head. With so much uncertainty, how should we make sense of approaching the poem today?

For some readers, *The Seafarer* is a rare and historical account of the brutal life at sea. To other readers, it is a literary and revelatory work in the tradition of wisdom poetry. To others again, it's a homily – its true journey being not one across oceans, but through the heavens toward God. Other readers have focused not on allegory but on the words *sylf* (self) and *anfloga* (lonely flying) as an early meditation of the soul in a manner that in later times we might call 'existential'. Others have pondered at the literary signature carried within: the marvellous word *forþon* – a word that pins the poem in no fewer than eight places – but a word for which no translators seem able to agree a meaning. What readers *do* agree upon is that the poem is uncommonly rich in poetic and metaphorical language, bearing one of the most rightly famed of all Anglo-Saxon kennings: *hwælweg*, literally *whale + way* or 'whale road', in other words: *the sea*.

Since I began translating Anglo-Saxon twenty years ago, *The Seafarer* has held a place in my regard so special that I vowed not to attempt it until I had enough experience of craft and life to make something of its depths. When Norman McBeath showed me his portrait of a bow wave, breaking fiercely on its dark self, its grained minutiae giving the appearance of a beast rising from below or some evolving form temporarily frozen at the surface by the camera lens, I thought at once of *The Seafarer*. At last, its tide had come towards me, as a collaborative current of word and image for this most lasting – and most *anfloga* – of poems.

MATTHEW HOLLIS

The Seafarer

THE TRANSLATION

MÆG IC BE ME SYLFUM soðgied wrecan,
siþas secgan, hu ic geswincdagum
earfoðhwile oft þrowade,
bitre breostceare gebiden hæbbe,
gecunnad in ceole cearselda fela,
atol yþa gewealc, þær mec oft bigeat
nearo nihtwaco æt nacan stefnan,
þonne he be clifum cnossað. Calde geþrungen
wæron mine fet, forste gebunden
caldum clommum, þær þa ceare seofedun
hat ymb heortan; hungor innan slat
merewerges mod.

COME, LEAN IN for this song of myself.
Bear with me these tides of telling.
Days without dawn, nights of no end,
the oceans upturning. I cannot calm
the surge within; I cannot stop the wave
from breaking: lost to the lookout,
watchful at prow, my keel-hand
shaking in the spill; driven too much
toward rocks. Cold to my cage,
my feet unfound, these bones a scaffold of frost;
then the starvation inside: mere-weary to core,
more worry than care.

Whoever settles
their days on land will never know the wintered waste,
the sheer alone, the friendless furrow,
cloaks of icicle, hail flown –
where nothing resounds, no stroke or beat,
but a hammer-sung sea, its weld of waves.
Swan song, sometimes, a whooper's wail,
the gannets' row – these for company, or the curlew
trying out its name – but nothing like the mirth of men:
gull-cry where once there was mead hall.
Storm there on stone. Storm there on stone.
Alone the ice-tipped terns answer, and, more
than once, an eagle out of ether, salt-
winged and sodden. But none like a friend.

And so
little they believe, who, cupped in life,
in the cradle of towns, washed
with wine, outlying unknown,
how worn in my seaway I remain.
Enfolding dark. Snow from the north.
Hail like the arrows of the earth,
till corn itself grows cold.

And so
how is it that the heart pulls harder:
draws me deeper onto towering seas;
commands me out to salt-break;
to go further in as I go further out;
guided by this spirit-guest, this unhoused host –
as if it alone held maps for where I'm going?

And so
where is a man on earth more self-aware,
more gifted or more fleet in youth,
or in his acts so sure, or with such watchful master,
that he embarks upon his journey without care
for what his true Master may confer.
No harp does he hear within, no dream of rings-received,
no wife with whom to warm, no hope on earth;
no rhythm to his mind but the pulsing sea,
a mark that no salt can scrub free.
Wood takes blossom, boroughs bloom,
meadows burden, spring hastens;
the cuckoo, that ward of summer,
unlocks a call from its chest-hoard:
Yu home. *Yu home.*
Each propels the quick and the driven,
those ready to journey, those who are given
to ocean paths on which they must one day depart;
how can landmen in their comfort know
the exile into which the oceaned go?

And so

my mood turns with the maul,
escapes, a moment, its locker of bones
to seek a threshold to the whale-world,
out on its tide and in again,
restless and keen:

lone-flyer,

soloist on the whale-road,
beyond the chorus of waters.

And so,

more lasting to me is this realm of reckoning
than the brief and barren life of land.

I do not believe

that wealth on earth endures.
Always, and without fail, one of three things
will clarify how the final hour will be:
sickness, old age or the sword
will call the one marked out for time.

And so
the only true test of any person
is how they are spoken of after they're gone:
that in their time they shall have acted well,
stood against wrongdoing, railed against indifference,
so that those who come after speak of them,
and in that way ensure their name on earth extends
beneath these skies, and finds a life unending
because it is carried among friends.
The days
fall through my fingers, the shore
recedes from sight. Neither kings
nor caesars, nor the gold-giving lords
remain of times before, when
they moved with glory and renown.
All now are gone; splendour is gone.
the world is left to the lesser, those
whose sentence is to toil.
Few are remembered;
dignity on earth is brought low
and every man is diminished.

Old age overtakes us, our countenance pales,
the heart greys with the hair; too many friends
have gone into the ground, each one born of higher hopes.
As to that, our own bodies too must fail,
till they know neither sunlight nor pain,
till the hand slows and the mind no longer responds.
Whether we gild the graves of brothers,
or hoard for our own passing,
gold stays only with the living,
and no amount can assuage a life misspent,
or assay the debt in the final account.

Fate kneels to no one; and so the earth must change,
secured on its sheet, well-founded
at four corners and in its skies above.
It is a fool who does not detect a greater calling:
he will be unprepared when the moment comes.
Humility is a gift; grace of light is a gift.
A measured heart is stable. And so with trust comes might.

~

We must fix our compass and keep it fixed,
live within trust, moderate our ways.
We shall temper friend and foe alike,
and though we will not wish suffering on any person,
least of all the friends we have made,
what happens is more than anyone can know.
Let us think where we may have our home,
and consider how we may reach it;
then strive to build a rapture that sustains,
inseparable from life, under love's direction,
hope without limit;
                                        indebted to the realm
in which we are raised,
                                           without beginning
                              or end.

The Seafarer

THE PHOTOGRAPHS

SEAFARER I

SEAFARER II

SEAFARER III

SEAFARER IV

SEAFARER V

SEAFARER VI

SEAFARER VII

SEAFARER VIII

SEAFARER IX

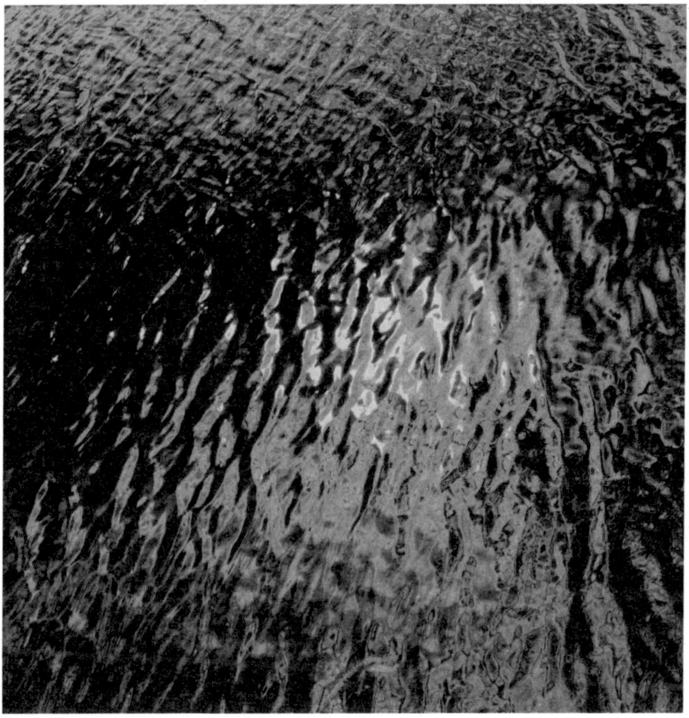

SEAFARER X

SEAFARER XI

SEAFARER XII

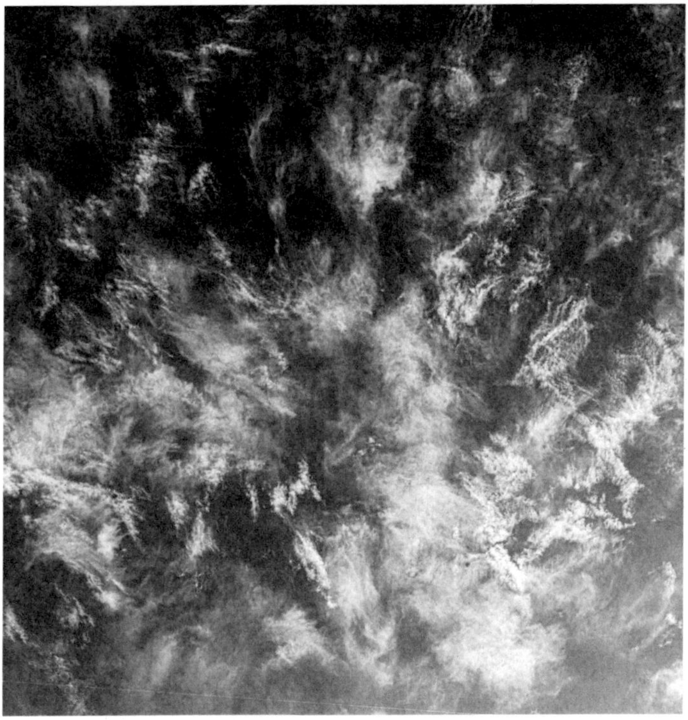

SEAFARER XIII

SEAFARER XIV

Afterword

On first reading the opening lines of Matthew's translation and interpretation of *The Seafarer,* I was instantly captivated by the salience of the words for our current times. The psychological depths revealed in such spare, strong language drew me in from the start. It acted like a catalyst on my subconscious, priming my vision, as I reviewed previous work and explored possible new themes and subjects.

It has always been a guiding principle for me in my collaborative work that any pairing of image and text should not be directly descriptive or explanatory. The words and images should always be able to stand on their own. When they are put together, they should bring different and additional possibilities of understandings to the reader and viewer. So the photographs I selected in response to Matthew's work are evocative, largely abstract in nature and open to multiple interpretations. I felt the photographs should be black and white as this would align more with an artistic approach, taking a step away from everyday perception and reinforcing the sense of the strange and mysterious that lies in the familiar all around us.

Norman McBeath RSA